COLORS & MARKINGS
OF THE
A-6
INTRUDER

C & M
VOL. 5

U.S. NAVY
BOMBER & TANKER VERSIONS

PART 1

A DETAIL & SCALE AVIATION PUBLICATION

D1613820

Bert Kinzey and Ray Leader

KALMBACH BOOKS

This book is a product of Detail & Scale, Inc., which has sole responsibility for its content and layout, except that all contributors are responsible for the security clearance and copyright release of all materials submitted. Published and distributed in the United States by TAB BOOKS Inc., and in Poole, Lane Cove, and Johannesburg by Arms and Armour Press.

CONTRIBUTORS:

Flightleader	Bob Stewart	Brian Pickering	Ian McPherson
Jerry Geer	Don Spering/AIR	Jim Leslie	Peter Thompson
L. Paul	Wayne Whited	Dwayne Kasulka	Werner Hartman
Ronald W. Harrison/Candid Aero Files	David F. Brown	Hugh Muir	Peter Berganini
George Cockle	Alan Landau	Kirt Minert	Don Logan
Donald McGarry	Douglas Slowiak	S. Matsuzawa	Brian Rogers
Michael Grove	Wallace T. Van Winkle	Akira Watanabe	Lindsay Peacock
Jim Sullivan	Jack Morris	Steve Daniels	Craig Kaston
Carlo Tripoli	Ben Knowles	Hideki Nagakubo	Grumman
David Ostrowski	L. B. Sides	John Binford	U.S. Navy

FIRST EDITION
FIRST PRINTING

Published in United States by

TAB BOOKS Inc.
P.O. Box 40
Blue Ridge Summit, PA 17214

Library of Congress Cataloging
in Publication Data

Kinzey, Bert.
A-6 Intruder.

(Colors & markings ; v. 5)
Companion vol. to: A-6 Intruder / by Bert Kinzey.
Blue Ridge Summit, PA : AERO, 1987. (Detail &
Scale ; v. 24).
1. Intruder (Bombers) I. Leader, Ray. II. Title.
III. Title; A6 Intruder. IV. Title: A-six Intruder.
V. Series: C & M ; vol. 5.
UG1242.B6K525 1987 623.74'63 87-1874
ISBN 0-8306-8529-4 (pbk.)

First published in Great Britain in 1987
by Arms and Armour Press
Limited, Link House
West Street, Poole, Dorset BH15111

Distributed in Australia by
Capricorn Link (Australia) Pty. Ltd.,
P.O. Box 665
Lane Cove, New South Wales 2066,
Australia

British Library Cataloging in
Publication Data

Kinzey, Bert.
A-6 Intruder. — (Colors & markings series ; 5)
1. Intruder (Bombers) 2. Airplanes,
Military — Identification marks
I. Title II. Series
623.74'63   UG1242.B6
ISBN 0-85368-799-4

Front cover: *This beautiful painting by aviation artist John Ficklen was painted specifically for the cover of this book. It depicts the launch of A-6E TRAM, 152915, on the mission on which it was lost over Lebanon on December 4, 1983. The pilot, LT Mark Lange, was killed, and the B/N, LT Robert Goodman was captured and held prisoner for a month. A great deal of research went into this painting to insure accuracy with respect to markings, paint scheme, ordnance load, correct catapult, weather, and flight deck conditions at the time of that particular launch. A limited series of numbered, collector's lithographs of this painting is being offered. Each print is autographed by LT Goodman and the artist, John Ficklen. All proceeds from the sale of these lithographs above the printing cost will go to a scholarship fund for LT Mark Lange's daughter, Jamie Lange. Information concerning ordering these lithographs may be obtained by writing to Detail & Scale, Inc., 256 Commerce Drive, Suite 432, Peachtree City, Georgia 30269.*

Rear cover: *This sign on the side of one of the hangars at NAS Oceana lets you know for sure just where you are. You're in INTRUDER COUNTRY!*
                                                                            (Kinzey)

INTRODUCTION

A-6A, 155718, from VA-115, and the **USS Midway** *is seen landing at NAF Atsugi in March 1974.*   *(Flightleader)*

Detail & Scale, Inc. is please to have acquired the Colors & Markings Series, and this volume is the first one to be released since this acquisition was made. It is being released as a companion volume to The A-6 Intruder in Detail & Scale, which covers the many details of the Intruder in the familiar Detail & Scale format.

The A-6 Intruder is known for its high degree of sophistication that enables it to attack targets in any weather, day or night. It has been around for a quarter of a century, and seems to get better with time. It is not known for its beautiful and sleek lines. Instead, it is considered something less than eye-appealing by many, but some of the more colorful paint schemes ever seen on military aircraft have been applied to it. Many of these are shown in the photos that appear on the pages of this book.

The scope of this book covers all U.S. Navy attack and tanker versions of the Intruder since the end of the war in Vietnam. Originally, we had planned to include the markings used during the Vietnam war, but the temporary assignments of Atlantic squadrons to Pacific carriers with Pacific tail codes, and the use of experimental camouflage schemes took up so much space that the Vietnam period is best left for another volume. Most markings carried in that time frame consisted mainly of two-letter tail codes, some special insignias, and very little in the way of colorful tail markings that began to adorn the aircraft just after the war. The electronic warfare versions of the A-6 will be covered in a future volume in the Colors & Markings Series, as will the Marine squadrons.

It is with the colorful post-war era that this book begins, and it looks at every Navy squadron on a unit-by-unit basis, ending with the markings carried in 1986. In that dozen years, the paint schemes and the markings carried by the Intruder and many other Naval aircraft have undergone a dramatic change. From color, to low-visibility, to the very subdued tactical schemes, all are shown here for each squadron. Dates are provided for most photographs so that the reader may understand the chronology of the change in markings. The photographs also provide an account of how some squadrons changed from one carrier air wing to another, with the resulting change in tail codes and carrier assignments.

Atlantic coast squadrons are covered first in numerical order, followed by Pacific coast squadrons. Test and evaluation aircraft for each coast are covered after the regular units for that coast. A brief introduction precedes the sections on each coast, and there is a short explanation of the evolution of the paint schemes and markings carried by A-6s during this time frame, but as always, photographs best cover this subject, and as much space is given to include as many of these photographs as possible. General overall photos are complimented by close-ups showing special markings, to include squadron insignia, markings used during the Bi-centennial celebration in 1976, and those used on CAG aircraft. Noteworthy are the photographs of the Libyan gunboat kills seen on page 30.

With the exception of the front cover, only photographs are used. No artist's paintings or line drawings are used, since actual photographs provide the best and most accurate record. However, a note is in order about the painting on the front cover. This painting was done specifically for this publication by the well-known aviation artist, John Ficklen. It illustrates the A-6E TRAM of VA-85 flown by LT Mark Lange, and LT Robert Goodman as it launched from the **USS John F. Kennedy** on December 4, 1983. The aircraft was shot down on this mission, resulting in the death of LT Lange, and the month-long captivity of LT Goodman, who was released in January 1984. The painting is based on considerable research by Detail & Scale, Inc., to include talks with LT Goodman, a study of the aircraft's maintenance records, and a photograph obtained from the U.S. Navy. It is accurate in every detail, to include the paint scheme and all markings, the ordnance load, and the catapult from which it was launched. We are indeed pleased to have this historically significant painting done for the cover by such an outstanding artist. A limited series of numbered, collector's lithographs of this painting is being offered. Each print is autographed by LT Goodman and the artist, John Ficklen. All proceeds from the sale of these lithographs above the printing cost will go to a scholarship fund for LT Mark Lange's daughter, Jamie Lange. Information concerning ordering these lithographs may be obtained by writing to Detail & Scale, Inc., 256 Commerce Drive, Suite 432, Peachtree City, Georgia 30269.

A-6 INTRUDER PAINT SCHEMES

A-6E, 149941, from VA-145, shows the typical post war scheme and colors applied to Intruders. The light gull gray over white scheme is evident, and colorful unit markings adorn the tail. Upper surfaces of the flaps, spoilers, and horizontal tail, as well as the rudder, are also white. Note the red inner surfaces of the flaps and speed brakes. This is standard for Intruders regardless of paint scheme.

(Flightleader)

The first Intruder prototype, then designated A2F-1, made its flight on April 19, 1960. At that time it was an unpainted bare metal with national insignias on the wings and aft fuselage, and the word **NAVY** was on the vertical tail. But it was soon painted in the light gull gray (FS 36440) over white scheme that was the Navy standard at that time. Upper surfaces of the horizontal stabilizer and control surfaces on the wings were also white. This scheme would remain the standard for the Intruder for over twenty years when the tactical low visibility scheme would replace it.

The first squadron to receive the A-6A Intruder was the Atlantic Fleet Readiness Squadron (FRS), which was VA-42. They were followed by VA-75, which was the first operational combat squadron, in 1964. VA-75 was also an Atlantic coast squadron based at Oceana NAS, and they were the first to take the Intruder into combat, followed by VA-85, and then VA-35. Since Atlantic coast squadrons received the Intruder before the Pacific coast units, the Atlantic squadrons were assigned to Pacific carriers and sent to the combat zone in Vietnam. While assigned aboard carriers in the Pacific, the Atlantic coast squadrons carried the appropriate tail code for the air wing assigned to that carrier. Pacific codes begin with the letter **N,** while Atlantic codes start with the letter **A.** Except for some unit insignia, these tail codes were the only unit markings carried by most squadrons during their tours in Vietnam. It would seem that the idea was that more important preparations for combat took priority over fancier and more colorful markings, so simplicity prevailed. The tail codes were often in two colors, one shading the other, but that was usually the extent of the color, save for an occasional tail band. For example, in 1965, VA-85 carried an NH tail code while operating aboard the **USS Kitty Hawk.** Later, in 1968, VA-85 carried an NK tail code in black, with a red tail band while aboard the **USS Constellation,** the same markings later carried by VA-196, which is a Pacific coast squadron. VA-65 carried the NH code aboard the **USS Kitty Hawk** in 1969.

By the time the war was over, both the Atlantic and Pacific coast squadrons were formed, and at the same time, the new A-6E was replacing the A-6A in these squadrons. It was at this time that colorful squadron markings began to appear on the Intruder. In most cases, these new markings were not as extensive as some seen during the same time on A-7 Corsairs, but they were, for the most part, considerably more colorful and imaginative than those seen during the war. This is where our coverage in this book begins.

The gray over white scheme with its colorful markings remained the standard for A-6 squadrons well into the late 1970s. In the 1977-78 time frame, an overall light gull gray replaced the gray over white on the F-14, the A-7, and a few other Navy aircraft to varying degrees. For the most part, this overall gray scheme did not replace the gray over white on Intruders. But the low visibility gray and black markings that began to appear with the overall gray scheme did begin to show up on Intruders that remained in the gray over white scheme. These low visibility markings removed a lot of the color from the A-6, but usually not all of it. For quite some time, extending well into the 1980s, Intruders did retain some color in the form of standard markings, national insignia, and even squadron markings to some extent. It was more of a toning down as far as the color was concerned, not an outright elimination of it. As late as 1983, a number of gray over white schemes could be seen on A-6s, and some color was present. But by mid-1984, the tactical paint scheme had taken over as the dominate scheme in Intruder Country.

Documenting the colors and markings involved with the tactical paint scheme for Intruders is almost an impossible task. In May 1984, when all but one Navy Atlantic coast A-6 squadron was ashore at their home base of NAS Oceana, Virginia, it was impossible to find more than two aircraft that were painted the same. Many aircraft had a two-tone tactical scheme consisting of FS 36302 and FS 36375. But any weathering would often blend these two shades

A-6A, 151782, from VA-85, and the **USS Kitty Hawk** *shows one of several short-lived camouflage schemes used during the Vietnam war. These camouflage schemes are the only variations from the gray over white and tactical schemes. This photo was taken in January 1965 off Yankee Station.* (Paul via Geer)

together. Other aircraft were painted in only one color, and others had three shades. A visit to a squadron maintenance area, and a look at aircraft records, showed that the Navy had directed that certain aircraft would be painted in specific tactical schemes that were assigned to the aircraft by BuNo. Aircraft came to the unit in the designated scheme, and unit markings applied by the squadron were supposed to be in certain specified colors. However, these were not always followed. Within any given squadron, tail codes and other markings could be found in flat black, dark gray, and blue gray. On two tone aircraft, markings were often in the opposite color to the background color on which the marking was painted. On one A-6, the tail was painted FS 36320, and the BuNo. was to be painted in FS 36375. However, a rectangle had been painted in FS 36375 instead, and the BuNo. was in FS 36320! Some aircraft had colorful insignia, others black ones, some gray ones, and in some cases there was a mixture of colors. Tail markings within any given unit, regardless of the subdued colors used, also varied considerably.

What all this means is that with the tactical paint schemes, there is no "standard" that can be applied to all A-6s in general. There are at least four schemes to be found

A-6E TRAM, 161106, from VA-55 illustrates the change to low visibility markings. Color still remains in the national insignia and other standard markings. Intruders retained the gray over white scheme when the change to low visibility markings was made instead of going to an overall gray scheme, as was the case with several other aircraft. (Harrison via Cockle)

in quantity, to include two of solid colors, a two-tone scheme, and a three-tone. Markings vary so much, even within a single unit at any given time, that it becomes impossible to say that one set of markings is THE unit markings for any particular squadron. Add to this the ever-changing air wing assignments and the resulting change in tail codes, and documentation of A-6 markings becomes a practical impossibility. To effectively do so would require an aircraft-by-aircraft record that would need many volumes to illustrate.

Most F-14 pilots seem to have been very upset with the loss of flash and color from their mounts as the low-visibility and tactical schemes replaced the original colorful markings. Perhaps time has lessened their distaste for the tactical schemes, but fighter jocks seem to have more of a flare for the colorful and flashy. Many argue that colorful and distinctive unit markings do a lot for the morale factor. But how do attack pilots and bombardier/navigators feel? Detail & Scale questioned a number of A-6 crewmembers, and all seemed very much in favor of the tactical scheme. In order to deliver ordnance against ground targets, the A-6 and other attack aircraft must fly slower than contemporary fighter aircraft. Their design speed is much slower, and being loaded with ordnance does not help. Therefore, attack pilots welcome anything that will help them survive in the combat arena, and the tactical paint schemes do help. Certainly it is better to fly an aircraft with a paint scheme that is less than eye-appealing and survive than it is to fly a colorful one and be shot down.

The tactical paint scheme is designed to increase survivability by making the aircraft harder to see, and also by reducing infrared reflectivity. But there remains the argument that some amount of color could be added to the tail, and could be quickly painted over if the need arose. Further, the need has also been expressed for a low-visibility paint that would stand up to the elements better, and that could be maintained in a nicer looking condition than the paint that is presently used. If such a paint, or a newer scheme, is found that will better enhance survivability, either by reducing the visual or infrared signature of the aircraft, we may see a new set of markings and schemes for the Intruder and many more combat aircraft.

One of the tactical paint schemes is shown here. This Intruder is painted in two tones of blue-gray, FS 36302 and FS 36375. The difference between the two shades is most visible on the radome and between the fairing behind the canopy and the fuselage. After some weathering, it becomes difficult to tell the demarcation between the two shades. (Cockle)

ATLANTIC COAST SQUADRONS

VA-65's early markings with orange "racing stripes" were one of the best known and most popular in the post-Vietnam period. This air-to-air shot shows the stripes to best advantage, including the area just behind the canopy. (Grumman)

There are eight Navy A-6 squadrons on the Atlantic coast. They are shore-based at NAS Oceana, Virginia, and are rotated in the air wings of the carriers assigned to the Atlantic fleet. As this is written, these assignments are in a state of constant change. The **USS Theodore Roosevelt** has just joined the fleet, and is temporarily working with Carrier Air Wing Seven. Air Wing Seven is actually assigned to the **USS Dwight D. Eisenhower,** which is presently in the yard for maintenance. When it returns in early 1987, Air Wing Seven will return to **Ike.** Carrier Air Wing One is expected to work on the **Roosevelt** after Air Wing Seven, but eventually Carrier Air Wing Eight, long the air wing of the **USS Nimitz,** will be assigned to the **Roosevelt.** The **USS Independence** is now in an extended yard period for the Service Life Extension Program (SLEP), and when it returns to duty, this former Atlantic coast carrier will be sent to the Pacific to replace the **USS Kitty Hawk,** which will be the next carrier to undergo the SLEP program.

In the past, the practice has usually been to assign one A-6 squadron to each carrier air wing, with the squadron consisting of both attack and tanker versions of the Intruder. However, dual A-6 air wings have existed, where one squadron has both attack and tanker versions, and the other has only the attack versions. Presently the **USS John F. Kennedy** has VA-75, and a Marine A-6 squadron, VMA (AW) 533, in its air wing. **USS Coral Sea** has both VA-55 and VA-65 in its air wing in a different configuration. Neither squadron has any tanker aircraft. Instead, each has about nine bomber versions. Tanker support is provided through the use of "buddy" store on the attack Intruders. This "Coral Sea Concept" may become the norm in the future, however, the Navy is currently looking at several air wing configurations, and shortly there may be no "standard" air wing. Already the F/A-18s are equipping both the fighter and former A-7 squadrons in the **USS Coral Sea,** and in the **USS Midway** in the Pacific. In other carriers they are only replacing the A-7s, with F-14s being in the fighter squadrons. These air wings will sometimes receive one, and other times two, A-6 squadrons.

Understanding the state of flux that the Atlantic A-6 squadrons are in, the following table lists the carriers and air wings to which each squadron is assigned. The list is current as of November 1986. In addition to these squadrons, our Atlantic coast coverage includes the Naval Air Test Center, Naval Air Test Facility, and the Naval Air Engineering Center.

SQUADRON NUMBER AND NAME	CARRIER AIR WING	CARRIER
VA-34 Blue Blasters	Seven	USS Dwight D. Eisenhower
VA-35 Black Panthers	Eight	USS Nimitz*
VA-42 Green Pawns	None	Atlantic Coast FRS
VA-55 Sea Horses	Thirteen	USS Coral Sea
VA-65 Tigers	Thirteen	USS Coral Sea
VA-75 Sunday Punchers	Three	USS John F. Kennedy
VA-85 Black Falcons	Seventeen	USS Saratoga
VA-176 Thunderbolts	Six	USS Forrestal

*To be reassigned to the USS Theodore Roosevelt in 1987.
Carrier Air Wing One is assigned to the USS America, but includes no A-6 squadron at present.
USS Independence is undergoing SLEP, and has no air wing assigned. It will go to the Pacific fleet once SLEP is completed.

VA-34 BLUE BLASTERS

Above: June 1976, markings for VA-34 are seen on KA-6D 152927, pictured at NAS Oceana. Note the Bi-centennial marking below the open canopy. There is no fuselage band to designate this aircraft as a tanker. At the time, the "Blue Blasters" were assigned to the **USS John F. Kennedy,** *and had an AB tail code.* (Flightleader)

Right: The Bi-centennial marking on the KA-6D shown in the photo above is seen here in detail. Also note the squadron marking on the fuel tank. (Flightleader)

Below left: One of the nineteen A-6As that were converted to A-6Bs is shown in this photo taken in June 1974. The nodes on the radome indicate that this is one of the -B conversions. Markings are the same as those in the photos above. However, there is no Bi-centennial marking. (Geer)

Below right: This close-up shows the details of the tail markings. But at the time this photo was taken in October 1977, the squadron had transferred to the **USS Dwight D. Eisenhower.** *The fact that the tail code did not change indicates that the entire air wing was moved to* **IKE.** (Flightleader)

Taken in May 1982, this A-6E TRAM from VA-34 is still in the gray over white scheme. This is the CAG aircraft, but carries no special markings. Note that the unit markings remain the same as those shown above on the tactical scheme, except that the national insignia is the large red, white, and blue style. The squadron is now assigned to the **USS America.** *(Flightleader)*

*Above left: This VA-34 KA-6D is painted in a one-tone tactical paint scheme in May 1981. This was one of the first tactical schemes, and is unusual in that colorful jet intake and rescue markings are still used. The national insignia and unit markings are all flat black. The tail band is dark blue, and the fuselage band is black. The unit is now reassigned to the **Kennedy**, as denoted by the carrier's name above the word **NAVY**.* *(Flightleader)*

*Above right: This view of the tail markings in November 1981 shows the small **AB** tail code on the rudder and the squadron name **BLUE BLASTERS** in white on a blue tail band. The aircraft number is at the top of the tail, and like the rest of the tail markings, is in black.* *(Flightleader)*

*No carrier name appears on this KA-6D as it taxis out for take-off at Offutt AFB on March 7, 1982. It is in the single-tone tactical scheme with black markings except for the intake, rescue, and danger markings. The **AB** tail code is retained.*
(Cockle)

These two photos are of the same aircraft, A-6E TRAM, 161667, and both photographs were taken in 1983. However, notice the change in markings. In the photo at left, taken in early 1983, the aircraft is in a worn, single-shade tactical scheme. Markings are a light blue-gray, and the nose number is flat black. At right, as photographed in October 1983, a two-tone gray scheme has been applied, with the lighter gray serving as markings on the darker gray and visa-versa. The nose number is in a darker gray as is the tail code and unit markings on the rudder. The positioning of the markings remains the same as in the photo at left.

(Left Flightleader, right Grove via Leader)

Also taken in 1983, these photos show two VA-34 Intruders still in the gray over white scheme. All markings are in a dark gray, except for the color that remains in the rescue, intake, and danger markings. All locations of markings remain the same as seen in the two photos above. Note the large Omega antenna on the spine of the KA-6D in the photo at right.

(Both Grove via Leader)

A weathered two-tone tactical scheme is seen on A-6E TRAM, 161679, as photographed in March 1985. The tail code is in a darker gray, but otherwise the two grays in the tactical scheme are used for markings on the opposite color. The nose number and crew names are also flat black. Note the formation light panel on the fuselage.

(Grove via Leader)

VA-35 BLACK PANTHERS

Above: VA-35's "Black Panthers" entered the post-war era with these markings as depicted on KA-6D, 151589. The unit was assigned to the **USS America**.

(Sullivan via Geer)

Left: The tail markings are seen in greater detail in this close-up. The circular outline around the disc is black, as is the panther within. The **AJ** tail code is a dark green. Note that the panther's legs on the rudder do not line up with the rest of the panther, indicating that the rudder came from another aircraft. (Flightleader)

Below: With its wings folded, A-6A, 151592, exhibits all of VA-35's markings to good effect. Note the difference in the anti-glare panel on this aircraft with the one on the aircraft at the top of the page. Fuel tank markings are in the same dark green as the **AJ** tail code. (Sullivan via Geer)

This interesting view of A-6E, 151592, on the flight deck of the **USS Nimitz** shows VA-35 markings in 1976. Careful examination of this photo will reveal a Bi-centennial tri-color **USS NIMITZ** on the fuselage. (Tripoli via Leader)

These two views show VA-35 markings in the 1977-80 time frame. Little has changed except that the **USS NIMITZ** is in black. The aircraft shown at right is the squadron commander's aircraft, and has crew names under the canopy rail.
(Left Flightleader, right Grove via Leader)

By May 1982, two changes had been made. The carrier to which the unit is assigned (temporarily) is the **USS Carl Vinson.** Second, the change to low visibility markings has started. While the national insignia and standard markings remain colorful, other markings are in black. The white disk is gone from the tail markings, and only the black circular outline remains. The **AJ** is also in black instead of the previous green, and although the aircraft is in the gray over white scheme, the rudder is no longer white.
(Cockle)

Above left: The change to the tactical scheme had begun for VA-35 in 1984, as seen here. Gone is the panther on the tail, and in fact, there are no unit markings on this aircraft. Although the paint is rather worn, this appears to be a single-color tactical scheme. (Grove via Leader)

Above right: Taken on the same day as the photo at left, this photograph shows a "Black Panther" KA-6D in the gray over white scheme. The tail code is low visibility gray, as is the nose number. Otherwise, the markings are the same as used by the unit when the disc and panther markings were used. (Grove via Leader)

Left: Two years later, the same KA-6D as seen above right is shown again. A panther has been added to the rudder in the same gray as used for the tail code. The nose number has been changed to 522. Also note the difference in the radome. (Ostrowski via Leader)

The CAG aircraft, 161668, appeared well worn on April 19, 1986. Note the change in colors in the replacement panels, and the poor appearance of the spot painting. The nose number is black, the tail code and panther are dark gray, and light gray is used for the remainder of the markings. (Ostrowski via Leader)

LIBYAN KILL MARKINGS

Above: VA-55 was one of the units to participate in the raids against Libya. A-6E TRAM, 161681, is seen here in the two-tone tactical scheme, with a dark gray tail code and sea horse. Under the canopy is a burning MiG-23 and a gunboat. The photo was taken in September 1986.

(Brown via Cockle)

Right: This close-up reveals details of the kill markings on the aircraft shown above. The gunboat is black, and colors for the burning MiG are shown below.(Brown via Cockle)

Below: A-6E TRAM, 159317's kill markings are seen in this detailed close-up photograph. No gunboat is present. The MiG is white with a red and yellow fire and black smoke.

(Landau via Leader)

VA-65 TIGERS

In 1974, VA-65 was assigned to the **USS Independence** and carried an **AG** tail code. Tail markings are orange outlined in black. The markings on the fuel tanks are also orange. Note that the orange "racing stripe" along the side of the fuselage (as seen on page 6) has now been deleted. There is no fuselage band to indicate that this is a tanker. *(Geer)*

VA-65's CAG markings are on 158531, as photographed on August 17, 1975. This aircraft is a factory-fresh A-6E, and is in mint condition. Although it is not as colorful as some Intruders have been, it still shows how much nicer the aircraft looks when maintained with a clean paint job. *(Flightleader)*

These two views show both sides of the tail on the CAG aircraft shown above. The stars above the scroll are in the various squadron colors. **CVW** is within the scroll, and **7** appears below it to indicate Carrier Air Wing Seven. Note the different locations of **USS INDEPENDENCE** on either side of the aircraft. *(Both Flightleader)*

Above: A Bi-centennial marking is on the rudder of KA-6D, 151818. The photograph was taken on July 31, 1976. Note the multiple ejector rack on this aircraft -- a rarity on a tanker.
(Flightleader)

Right: Another tanker, 152611, is shown in this photograph that was taken at NAS Oceana on October 20, 1977. The orange fuselage band is outlined in black. **USS INDE-PENDENCE** *is just above the word* **NAVY** *in black.*
(Flightleader)

Below: Also photographed in 1977, A-6E, 155674, shows the standard VA-65 markings of that time period.
(Flightleader)

Two changes are noteworthy in this photograph as compared to those on the preceding page. First, the transition to low visibility markings has begun. A staggered **AG** appears on the tail with a tiger in between the letters. The second change is that the squadron has now been assigned to the **USS Dwight D. Eisenhower.** A laser guided bomb of the training variety is seen under the left wing. *(Grove via Leader)*

On A-6E TRAM, 161083, the tail codes and tiger are in black, and the aircraft remains in a well maintained gray over white scheme. At right is a close-up showing the details of the tiger marking on the tail. *(Left Grove via Leader, right Kinzey)*

Pale gray is used for the **AG** tail code and tiger on 154135. Otherwise the markings remain the same as those seen above. The photograph was taken in April 1984. *(Harrison via Cockle)*

This photograph was also taken in April 1984, and by comparison to the photo at left, shows a change in tail markings. The tail code is gray, and is now horizontal rather than being offset as seen at left and above. The tiger is the same design as before, but has been moved to the rudder. *(Grove via Leader)*

The change to tactical schemes for VA-65 is the subject of this page. Note the different grays used for the markings on this aircraft. The numbers on the nose and the top of the tail are in black. The tiger on the rudder is almost invisible.

(Grove via Leader)

This is the CAG aircraft for VA-65 in 1984. The BuNo. is 151804, although this is almost invisible on the tail. As is sometimes the case, the TRAM turret and the plate around it are white.

(Slowiak via Cockle)

The right side of the CAG aircraft is shown here. The tiger is more visible on the rudder in this photo. The national insignias on the fuselage and tail are almost invisible here as well as in the photo above.

(Kinzey)

This close-up of the tail of a VA-65 Intruder in the tactical scheme better illustrates the details of the tiger on the rudder. Note that it has an outline around it.

(Kinzey)

21

VA-75 SUNDAY PUNCHERS

VA-75 entered the post-war period with an all white tail with blue and yellow flashes. An oriental style tail code is in black. This is the CAG aircraft, photographed in June 1974, and squadron colors are represented on the rudder. This A-6A has an interesting marking on the intake. It is in the shape of a diamond with a large **1** and smaller **VA-75** within. *(Geer)*

Markings remain the same in this color shot taken at Dobbins AFB on December 19, 1976. Note the colors in the squadron insignia on the fuselage near the canopy. *(Flightleader)*

Although not in color, this view shows the details of the squadron marking better than the general photographs. It was on both sides of the fuselage. *(Flightleader)*

Dark blue and yellow bands wrap around the aft fuselage of this VA-75 tanker. Left side details of the unit's markings are also revealed. *(Harrison via Geer)*

Color is still visible, but less predominate than on the aircraft seen on the previous page. The all-white tail is gone, with only the rudder remaining in white. **USS SARATOGA** is in smaller letters, and the squadron insignia has been deleted. This photo is dated January 1981, and was taken at Tyndall AFB, Florida.

(Flightleader)

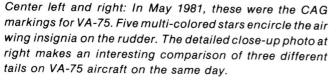

Center left and right: In May 1981, these were the CAG markings for VA-75. Five multi-colored stars encircle the air wing insignia on the rudder. The detailed close-up photo at right makes an interesting comparison of three different tails on VA-75 aircraft on the same day.

(Both, Flightleader)

Right: A low visibility tail code and unit markings appear in the late 1981 on this A-6E TRAM. The winged bomb, in several styles, became the squadron marking for the "Sunday Punchers" in this time frame.

(Van Winkle)

Above left: Complete low-visibility markings are on this KA-6D, and a change in the tail markings is noteworthy. The winged bomb is now much smaller and is located on the rudder. All markings are in gray except for the nose number and the usual warning and rescue markings.
(Stewart via Leader)

Above right: The same markings as on the aircraft at left are on this tanker, except that the colorful insignia is used. Note that the squadron had been moved to the **USS John F. Kennedy** by the time that this photograph was taken in September 1985. Fuel tanks are painted in the tactical blue-gray. *(Grove via Leader)*

Left: A slight variation in markings is seen on yet another tanker belonging to VA-75. The standard markings used on the gray over white scheme are used except for the tail code, which is gray, and the winged bomb on the rudder. Here the winged bomb is black, and has a circle surrounding it. Two-tone tactical tanks are on the pylons.
(Grove via Leader)

A-6E TRAM, 161660, shows the effects of fading from the weather on the tactical scheme. Effects of spot painting are also clearly visible. The aircraft was just beginning to fold its wings when this photograph was taken in September 1985.
(Grove via Leader)

VA-85 BLACK FALCONS

VA-85 is one of the better known A-6 squadrons. It served tours in Southeast Asia, flew combat in Lebanon, and most recently was involved in the raids against Libya. This KA-6D, 151572, shows the squadron's markings in February 1974. Note the falcon on the tail, representing the unit's name, "Black Falcons." *(Flightleader)*

Right: Dated October 10, 1974, this photo shows A-6E, 158797. The **E** *excellence award is under the canopy. The radome is a cream white, which was fairly standard during this time period. Earlier, radomes were often black, and were later painted gray over white.* *(Morris via Leader)*

Below: On February 28, 1976, two noteworthy changes can be seen. First the falcon on the tail has been colored to observe America's Bi-centennial celebration, and second, the green band has been removed from the tail.

(Flightleader)

Bi-centennial colors carried over into 1977 as this photograph, taken on April 29th of that year illustrates. The multi-colored tail markings of the CAG aircraft are clearly visible as the two aircraft make their approach into NAS Oceana.

(Flightleader)

By late October 1977, the standard falcon marking was back in style, replacing the Bi-centennial colors. This is A-6E, 158050.

(Flightleader)

CAG A-6E, 158793, had the standard falcon on the tail when it was photographed at Dobbins AFB, Georgia, on February 2, 1978.

(Flightleader)

Center: KA-6D, 151582, came with the CAG aircraft above on its stopover at Dobbins. Note the green fuselage band.
(Flightleader)

Right: An early production A-6A, later converted to an A-6E, is shown on the receiving line at Davis Monthan. The number on the intake is the number given the airframe at Davis Monthan. The radome on this aircraft is a glossy off-white instead of the more predominate cream white.
(Knowles via Leader)

By 1980, a beginning to the move toward low visibility is indicated on A-6E, 158528. This is the CAG aircraft, and far less color is used than on the multi-colored rudder seen previously.
(Grove via Leader)

Center left and right: As the transition continues, gray replaces black for many of the markings on the aircraft at left. The nose number, BuNo., USS FORRESTAL, and VA-85 are all in gray. Note the lack of a lightning bolt in the AA tail code. Also notice the differences in radomes. At right, a KA-6D has most of the same markings in black, and the lightning bolt is present. *(Both Cockle)*

Left: By February 1983, some of VA-85's aircraft had been painted in the two-tone tactical paint scheme. The markings remain basically the same, and the unit is still assigned to the USS FORRESTAL. *(Grove via Leader)*

After many years of flying from the **USS Forrestal,** VA-85 was moved to the **USS John F. Kennedy.** In 1983, it began the cruise that included the action over Lebanon. The photos on this page were taken very shortly after the unit returned from that cruise. Almost all of the squadron's aircraft were painted in a tactical scheme consisting of but one color. However, the same color was not used on every aircraft. Tail markings, insignias, the BuNo., and the carrier's name were in light gray, medium gray, a blue-gray, and black, but were all the same style and in the same location. Note the unusual radome colors on this aircraft.

(Kinzey)

Three different colors for tail markings are visible in these two photographs. At left, light gray is used, while dark gray is used for the tail code and falcon in the photo at right. In the background is an aircraft with black markings. It remains in the gray over white scheme, however, some other aircraft in the tactical scheme also had black markings. (Both Kinzey)

As late as mid-1984, a few A-6E TRAMs still remained in the gray over white scheme. These two photos show both sides of 154136 in May 1984.

(Both, Kinzey)

LIBYAN GUNBOAT KILL MARKINGS

Above: The **AC** tail code gave way to a return to **AA** for the "Black Falcons". However, this time the squadron and Carrier Air Wing Seventeen were assigned to the **USS Saratoga.** They saw action in the raids against Libya, and achieved some measure of success as the kill markings on this page indicate. This is A-6E TRAM, 161662, and a small single kill marking is visible just under the aft portion of the canopy.

Left: This is a close-up view of the gunboat kill marking on the aircraft shown above.

Below: A-6E, 161685, the squadron commander's aircraft has two gunboat kills.

(All photos on this page, Ostrowski via Leader)

VA-176 THUNDERBOLTS

VA-176 entered the post-Vietnam era in A-6As, and was assigned to the **USS Franklin D. Roosevelt.** The squadron is called the "Thunderbolts," and unit markings include a fist with a lightning bolt on the tail. At left is A-6A, 157001, in June 1974, and at right is KA-6D, 152592, as photographed in July 1975. Note the name **USS ROOSEVELT** on the fuselage. Six blue stars appear at the base of the rudder on both aircraft.

(Left Geer, right Sides via Leader)

Right: By 1976, VA-176 was moved to the **USS America,** as the **FDR** was scheduled for decommissioning. **USS AMERICA** appears on the fuselage, and is visible just above the wing. Also note the red, white, and blue streamer on the fuselage in recognition of America's Bi-centennial celebration. The squadron insignia is located just forward of it.

(Pickering via Leader)

Below: A-6E, 154171, is shown in color as of January 1977. The lightning bolt is in red with a thin black outline. The Bi-centennial streamer and squadron insignia are no longer on the fuselage.

(Flightleader)

Above: VA-176 began 1978 still assigned to the **USS America** and wearing the same markings it had carried since its days on the **FDR.** This photo shows A-6E, 154126, at NAS Oceana on May 11, 1978.   (Flightleader)

Left: Although this is VA-176's CAG aircraft, 158796, it shows no special markings as it makes its landing approach.   (Flightleader)

Below: By the end of 1978, as seen in this photo taken in November, the squadron had moved to the **USS Independence,** still wearing the same markings it had used in 1974. This is a tanker, and it has a diagonal fuselage band instead of the more common vertical one.   (Harrison via Geer)

By 1980 the change to low visibility markings had begun for VA-176. The **AE** tail code and lightning bolt are light gray on this aircraft, and the fist of armor that previously held the lightning bolt is now gone. Note the Vulcan bomber in the background.

(Cockle)

The next change in markings for VA-176 is seen in this 1983 photo. The lightning bolt is now gone entirely, and most markings are a subdued medium gray. The **AE** tail code is now horizontal rather than being offset.

(Cockle)

Both taken in 1985, these two photos show similar markings on two different schemes. The A-6E TRAM, 155687, seen at left is the CAG aircraft, and although it is hard to see, the armored fist with the lightning bolt has returned as a small marking on the rudder. Note the small gray national insignia under the right wing. At right, the gray over white scheme remains on KA-6D, 152592, and it has the same markings to include the fist and lightning bolt on the rudder. The markings are in a darker gray than on the tactical scheme seen at left. Tankers were often the last aircraft to be painted in the new scheme, and official directives still call for tankers to be painted in the gray over white scheme. Individual units have painted them in the tactical scheme in many cases.

(Left Flightleader, right Harrison via Cockle)

TEST & EVALUATION INTRUDERS (ATLANTIC)
NAVAL AIR TEST CENTER

Above and center: The Naval Air Test Center is located at NAS Patuxent River, Maryland. Up until the 1975 time frame, directorates were separated according to functions. The photo at the top of the page illustrates the "Service Test" function, and has a stylized S on the tail. Tail, outer wing panels, and intakes are day-glow orange. The S is black with a white outline. The remains of a chevron are visible under the S. The chevron marking is used for the "Flight Test" function. At center a white W on the tail represents the "Weapons System Test" function.

(Top Geer, center Ostrowski via Leader)

Left: After 1975, a "Flight Directorate" and a "Strike Directorate" combined the functions for different types of aircraft. Naturally, the A-6 falls under the "Strike Directorate." The NATC badge replaced the previous W, S, and chevron markings on both sides of the tail. *(Flightleader)*

By April 1977, the Strike Aircraft Test badge replaced the NATC badge on the left side of the tail, while the NATC insignia remained on the right side. NATC colors are shown to good effect here. (Flightleader)

These two close-ups show the NATC (left) and Strike Aircraft Test insignias on the tails of two Intruders. **NAVAL AIR TEST CENTER** *appears on both sides.* (Both, Flightleader)

A-6E, 154131, and A-6E TRAM, 159567, are shown in the tactical scheme during the 1984-86 time frame. The day-glow orange remains on the tail, wings, and intakes. **7T,** *which is the station code for Pax River, has been added to the tail. On the aircraft at left it is black, shadowed in white, while at right it is in black with no shadow.* (Both Flightleader)

A-6E TRAM PROTOTYPE

Special prototype test aircraft are also flown at NATC. This is the prototype A-6E TRAM, 155673, in a flashy Grumman scheme. It is overall white with red, white, and blue markings.
(Grumman)

For the majority of the time the aircraft was undergoing testing, it wore this rather standard scheme with a special TRAM marking on the tail. This photo was taken on February 21, 1975, at NAS Patuxent River.
(Flightleader)

This is another view of the TRAM prototype. Earlier, this same airframe had served as the A-6E prototype, being converted from an A-6A.
(Flightleader)

This close-up reveals details of the TRAM insignia. It consists of a TRAM turret at the top of a disc. Peering out of the turret is a cartoon character with a flashlight in one hand, and he is pointing, as if to a target, with the other hand. Colors are more apparent in the photo above.
(Flightleader)

NAVAL AIR TEST FACILITY

*A-6A, 149940, is seen here in May 1977, in the markings of the Naval Air Test Facility at Lakehurst, N.J. The day-glow orange markings are the same as those seen on NATC aircraft. A white disc appears on the tail with a chevron and **NATF Lakehurst** within.*

(Stewart via Leader)

NAVAL AIR ENGINEERING CENTER

Above center: Taken in March 1978, this photograph shows the change to the Naval Air Engineering Center (NAEC), still located at Lakehurst. Note that this is the same aircraft as seen above one year earlier. *(Leslie via Leader)*

Right: The right side of the same aircraft is shown here. Tail markings are the same on both sides. *(Flightleader)*

PACIFIC COAST SQUADRONS

VA-128 is the Fleet Readiness Squadron for the Pacific Intruder units. This is 152628, a KA-6D from that squadron, and it was photographed on October 24, 1982. *(Cockle)*

The "Knight Riders" of VA-52 marked their Intruders with a blue knight's helmet and lance in the more colorful days of Intruder markings. Pacific coast units have tail codes that begin with N instead of the A used by Atlantic squadrons. *(Cockle)*

Seven Intruder squadrons are assigned to the Navy's Pacific Air Fleet. VA-128 is the Pacific Fleet Readiness Squadron. The other six units are assigned to the six carriers that operate in the Pacific. Their shore base is NAS Whidbey Island, Washington, except for VA-115, which is assigned to the **USS Midway.** Since **Midway** is based at Yokosuka, Japan, being the only U.S. carrier with a home port other than in the United States, its air group is also shore-based in Japan. VA-115 has a home base of NAF Atsugi. There are presently no dual A-6 air wings as there are in the Atlantic fleet. One squadron is assigned to each carrier, and both attack and tanker versions of the Intruder are currently in each squadron. The following table summarizes the air wing and carrier assignments of the Pacific Fleet Intruder units as of November 1986.

SQUADRON NUMBER AND NAME	CARRIER AIR WING	CARRIER
VA-52 Knight Riders	Fifteen	USS Carl Vinson
VA-95 Sky Knights	Eleven	USS Enterprise
VA-115 Chargers	Five	USS Midway
VA-128 Golden Intruders	None	Pacific Coast FRS
VA-145 Swordsmen	Two	USS Ranger
VA-165 Boomers	Nine	USS Kitty Hawk
VA-196 Main Battery	Fourteen	USS Constellation

VA-52 KNIGHT RIDERS

The VA-52 CAG aircraft is seen in this photograph which was taken at NAS North Island in October 1977. The plume in the knight's helmet has the various colors of the air group's squadrons in it. On other aircraft, the plume is the same blue as the helmet.

(Flightleader)

Center left and right: One attack Intruder and one tanker illustrate the standard VA-52 markings in these two photos. The tanker has a blue fuselage band. The knight's lance is on some fuel tanks and not on others.

(Left Grove via Leader, right Flightleader)

Right: A close-up of the standard aft fuselage and tail markings of VA-52 is seen here. **USS KITTY HAWK** and the **NH** tail code are black. Note that the red light on the leading edge of the vertical tail serves as the eye for the helmet.

(Flightleader)

A-6E TRAM, 155637, is still in full colors in January 1979. The notable change here from the photos on the previous page is that the tail code has changed to **NL.** It is black, shadowed in white. The carrier remains the **USS Kitty Hawk.**

(Flightleader)

A-6E TRAM, 155632, is seen in standard VA-52 markings on March 5, 1982. The aircraft appears in exceptionally well maintained condition.

(Cockle)

Compare the **NL** tail code on this aircraft to the one in the photo immediately above. It is not as high, and is thicker. This excellent take-off shot was taken at Offutt AFB, Nebraska, on July 18, 1982.

(Cockle)

Also taken in 1982, this photograph shows one of the first VA-52 aircraft to be painted in a tactical scheme. This is a recently painted aircraft, and examination of the markings will reveal that the knight's helmet and lance are still used. **USS KITTY HAWK** still appears above the word **NAVY**.

(Grove via Leader)

In 1983 the gray over white scheme still remained on some VA-52 aircraft as exemplified by these two photographs. What is more important here is that the squadron has now been assigned to the **USS Carl Vinson**. Otherwise the markings have not changed.

(Both Cockle)

The first real change in VA-52 markings is seen here in late 1985. The **NL** tail code is offset, and no helmet or lance is used.

(Grove via Leader)

This tactical scheme appeared on 161680, in June 1985. The lance is gone, but the helmet still remains on the tail.

(Grove via Leader)

VA-95 SKY KNIGHTS

A-6A, 154134, from the "Sky Knights" of VA-95, was photographed at NAS Miramar in September 1974. The tail band is green, and the **NL** is black. The unit was assigned to the **USS Coral Sea.** (Kasulka via Geer)

By 1975, more color had been added to the tail. A green trident passes through the black **NL** tail code which is now horizontal rather than being offset. Notice the difference in the anti-glare panel as compared to the one in the photograph above. This photograph was taken on November 1, 1975. (Muir via Leader)

Above: While the markings remain basically the same as shown on the previous page, there are two important changes seen on A-6E, 155597. First the unit has moved to the **USS America,** and second, the tail code has changed to **NH.** A lesser change is the markings on the fuel tanks. Compare these with the markings on the tanks in the photo at the bottom of the previous page. Also note the off-white radome. *(Flightleader)*

Right: By 1980, new markings had appeared on the tail. The stylized trident is now in the hands of a sea dragon. The **NH** tail code is vertical on the rudder, and the carrier remains the **USS America.** *(Minert via Leader)*

Right side markings and colors are seen on A-6E, 159895, as photographed in November 1980. *(Grove via Leader)*

By 1981, the sea dragon had disappeared from the tail, and perhaps the most non-descript markings to appear on the gray over white scheme remain, consisting of only the black NH tail code. Except for the **VA-95** on the side of the fuselage, and the **506** nose number, this aircraft could have just come off of the production line. Note the white radome.   (Cockle)

Several differences are noteworthy here when compared to the photo above. First, there is the presence of a green band at the top of the vertical tail. The radome is in the gray over white scheme, and this is a tanker with a green fuselage band. **USS AMERICA** appears on the fuselage. Note the differences in the anti-glare panel compared to that seen above. In both cases, the in-flight refueling probe is flat black instead of the usual gray.   (Cockle)

Low visibility markings are apparent in this photo dated September 1983. The **NH** tail code is very small and back, being located on the vertical tail instead of the rudder. The green band is gone. Colorful insignias and standard markings remain on this A-6E TRAM. The squadron is now assigned to the **USS Enterprise.**   (Grove via Leader)

By September 1983, 161666, had been painted in the two-tone tactical scheme. Markings remain the same and in the same locations as seen at left, but they are all subdued grays and black.   (Grove via Leader)

44

Even by 1985, not all of VA-95's aircraft had been painted in the tactical scheme. At left is the CAG aircraft, photographed in May 1985, and notice how the old markings seem to be making a comeback. The trident has reappeared on the tail, and the green band is on the fin cap. At right, KA-6D, 149936, has similar markings, but the band is not present at the top of the tail. A green fuselage band is present. The fuel tanks are in the tactical scheme. (Both Grove via Leader)

Taken on April 20, 1985, A-6E TRAM, 158533, is seen in the tactical scheme. In a commendable attempt to liven it up, VA-95 has added a shadowed trident marking and **NH** to the tail. (Flightleader)

The right side markings of the same aircraft as pictured above are seen in this photograph. (Grove via Leader)

VA-115 CHARGERS

Some of the most colorful markings ever to be carried by the Intruder were the early markings of VA-115, assigned to the **USS Midway.** Here, KA-6D, 151824, is photographed on final approach into NAF Atsugi, Japan, on May 28, 1975. Note the markings on the fuel tanks. (Matsuzawa via Leader)

This A-6A from VF-115 was photographed at Iwakuni MCAS, Japan in August 1976. Colors are the same as seen above and below. (Wanatabe via Geer)

The colorful CAG aircraft for VA-115 is seen on the flight deck of the **USS Midway** in March 1976. Modelers should note that this is the aircraft and these are the markings represented by one set of decals in the Hasegawa 1/72nd scale A-6A kit. (Daniels via Leader)

By 1977, the dark blue tail had disappeared, and the style of the **NF** tail code had changed. Otherwise the markings are similar to those seen on the previous page. This is KA-6D, 151796, and it was photographed on June 9, 1977.

(Nagakubo via Leader)

One of the early A-6As that were converted to A-6Es, is seen on the receiving line at Davis-Monthan on May 1, 1980. It did not receive the TRAM conversion. The Davis-Monthan inventory number is on the intake. (Cockle)

A-6E, 155588, was photographed on June 30, 1981, still in the gray over white scheme. (Cockle)

VA-128 GOLDEN INTRUDERS

Above: The "Golden Intruders" of VA-128 are the Fleet Readiness Squadron for the Pacific coast. Until the introduction of the tactical scheme, shown on the next page, their markings changed little from those illustrated in this photograph. (Flightleader)

Left: Bi-centennial markings were added to the rudder of VA-128 aircraft in 1976, as part of the two-hundredth birthday celebration for the United States. Other markings remain the same as those seen above.
(Stewart via Leader)

Below: A-6E TRAM, 155673, was photographed on the transit line at Offutt AFB, on January 28, 1983. The **00** nose number would indicate a commander's aircraft, but not in the same sense as the CAG aircraft of squadrons assigned to air wings. Fleet Readiness Squadrons, or RAGs (Replacement Air Groups) are not assigned to carrier air wings. (Cockle)

Even in 1984, after other squadrons had gone to at least the low visibility markings, and mostly to the tactical schemes, some VA-128 Intruders still carried full colors on the gray over white scheme. Noteworthy on this aircraft is the unusual anti-glare panel that extends up on to the windscreen framing.

(Cockle)

Right: By 1985, the change to the tactical scheme for VA-128 had caused a change in markings. The winged **1** is still on the tail, as is the **NJ** tail code. This rather worn A-6E TRAM was photographed in June 1985.

(Binford via Leader)

Below: Three shades of tactical blue-grays are visible on this aircraft. It appears that this aircraft is more recently painted and/or better maintained than the one shown above. VA-128 was able to keep its standard markings the same basic design during the transition to the tactical scheme, although they are lacking any of the previous color.

(Grove via Leader)

VA-145 SWORDSMEN

As VA-145 entered the post-Vietnam era, it was equipped with A-6As and KA-6Ds in these markings. These two photos both show tanker aircraft. The photo at left was taken in January 1974, and the one on the right is dated July 1975. At that time the unit was assigned to the air wing aboard the **USS Ranger**.   (Left Geer, right Flightleader)

VA-145's "Swordsmen" painted a green and yellow sword on the tail under the **NE** tail code. Its colors are evident in this photo, as is the Bi-centennial emblem on the fuselage side. The photo was taken in October 1976. (Grove via Leader)

This is the CAG aircraft for VA-145 in January 1980. The multi-colored sword is representative of the squadron colors in the air wing.   (Grove via Leader)

KA-6D, 151808, has a green fuselage band in addition to the other VA-145 markings.   (Grove via Leader)

Above: A complete change in tail markings can be seen in this November 1980 photograph, taken aboard the **USS Coral Sea** while the carrier was in port. A buddy refueling store is on the centerline station. (Grove via Leader)

Right: Right side markings are seen on KA-6D, 151576, which was photographed in October 1980. Note that **CVW14** is stenciled on the fuselage speed brake even though this is not a CAG aircraft. It does not appear on the A-6E TRAM shown above. Surprisingly enough, it is not on the CAG aircraft in the bottom photo either. The squadron marking also remains behind the canopy on this aircraft. (Grove via Leader)

Another CAG aircraft is shown here in the new markings for VA-196. The large overlapping spades are used on the rudder again. This is the same aircraft seen with the overlapping spades on the previous page. (Grove via Leader)

The change to low visibility markings is evident in this photograph of KA-6D, 151576, taken on May 30, 1982. The tail and fuselage bands are red-orange with a thin black outline. Except for the fact that the **NK** tail code is much smaller, these markings are practically the same as the unit's original markings. Again, note the **CVW 14** on the speed brake.(Cockle)

The markings remain the same on this A-6E TRAM, but the carrier is now the **USS Constellation.** This is the CAG aircraft, and it has several colors at the aft end of the thin tail band. They are small and subtle, not showing up well in a photograph of this size. This photograph was taken in September 1984.   (Grove via Leader)

In June 1985, the tail markings were changed considerably. The **NK** tail code is offset, and a black spade has been added. The tail and fuselage bands are also black.
(Grove via Leader)

The two-tone tactical scheme was used on many VA-196 Intruders by September 1984, when this photograph was taken. Note that the style and location of the tail code and band is like that seen in the photo at the top of this page and at center left.
(Grove via Leader)

TEST & EVALUATION INTRUDERS (PACIFIC)
VX-5

A-6E, 152593, has the AIRTEVRON FIVE (VX-5) badge on both sides of the vertical tail. A close-up of the marking is at right. The insignia is basically black and yellow, with red and blue in with the yellow for the colors in the bottom portion of the disc. The moons are white. These photos were taken on November 13, 1975, at China Lake. (Both, Peacock via Leader)

*These two Intruders have the better known VX-5 markings, consisting of a wide green band outlined in white, with an **XE** tail code. The fin cap is white. Note the VX-5 marking on the right fuel tank in the photograph at right. The style and position of the BuNo. is different on these two aircraft. The photo at left was taken on May 15, 1980, and the one at right is dated July 9, 1982.* (Both, Cockle)

*This Intruder was photographed in VX-5 markings on February 19, 1983, at NAS Alemeda. The white tail band is gone, as is the **S** award marking on the rudder. This aircraft was an early A-6A, and has now been brought up to A-6E TRAM standards.* (Grove via Leader)

Naval Missile Center markings adorn the tails of all types of aircraft operated by that facility. Above is A-6A, 151784, and below is 151784. These markings remained unchanged until NMC became the Pacific Missile Test Center, which is covered next. Noteworthy is the red marking on the fuel tank in the bottom photo.   (Top Muir via Leader, bottom Flightleader)

PACIFIC MISSILE TEST CENTER

Right: The Pacific Missile Test Center is located at Point Mugu, California. It performs developmental tests and evaluations as well as training support for naval weapons systems. Its triangular shaped marking is seen on the tail of KA-6D, 149484. The tail is red-orange, being left over from a former assignment at NATC. This photo is dated May 11, 1978. (Flightleader)

Below center: The blue tail band and the colors of the PMTC insignia are illustrated in this color photograph, taken in December 1981. Note the same markings on a P-3 in the background. (Grove via Leader)

Both sides of A-6E, 152642, are seen in these two photographs. Except for the blue band, PMTC insignia, and nose number, all markings are standard Intruder markings that are on the aircraft at the time a unit receives the aircraft.(Both, Cockle)

NAVAL WEAPONS CENTER, CHINA LAKE

The Naval Weapons Center is located at China Lake, California. It conducts flight and firing test of air-to-ground and air-to-air weapons. A-6A, 149937, is in the gray over white scheme in May 1977, and it has an unusual gray radome. At right, A-6E, 159569, has similar markings except that it also has a white fin cap on the tail, and **NWC** above **CHINA LAKE** on the tail. This photo was taken as ground crew personnel loaded 500 pound high drag bombs.

(Left Flightleader, right Berganini via Leader)

This A-6E TRAM, 159569, is in the two-tone tactical scheme with new NWC markings on the tail. The aircraft has 500 pound bombs and a Harpoon missile under the right wing. *(Kaston via Leader)*

NAVAL WEAPONS EVALUATION FACILITY

Left: The Naval Weapons Evaluation Facility at Albuquerque, New Mexico, assists in establishing and maintaining special weapons capability with Navy combat aircraft. This A-6A, 149953, has the Indian style eagle on the tail, and NWEF below it. This has been the standard marking for the facility for many years, and remains on their aircraft today.

(Flightleader)